JUST MOMMY AND ME

Written by Eleanor Pinney

Illustrated by Mayhara Ferraz

Dedication

My mommy and I do everything together. I love her so much! We have a lot of fun cooking dinner. I get the seasoning from the cupboard so she can make my favorite dish: chicken and rice and peas with corn and carrots on the side.

My mom also makes carrot juice, a famous Jamaican tradition that nourishes my body to keep me strong and healthy. Carrots are also good for your eyes!

My mommy helps me with my homework,
so I do well in school and get good grades. We
read every night, and my mom teaches me about
extraordinary Black leaders like Rosa Parks,
Harriet Tubman, Ruby Bridges, Martin Luther King,
Nelson Mandela, and Viola Desmond. These people
have paved the way for Black people. We also
practice my addition, subtraction, multiplication,
and division so that I can develop my math skills.
My mother always stresses the importance of
getting a good education.

My mommy combs, cornrows my hair and puts beads at the ends. When I walk, my beads make music. The beat reminds me of a reggae and soca festival, where we rock our hips, snap our fingers, and hold a vibez with the people in our community. My mom is creative with my hair. She puts zigzag parts, ponytails, and extensions in my hair. I get a lot of compliments from my teachers and friends at school.

My mommy takes me to the doctor and dentist to stay healthy and strong. Mommy holds my hand when I am scared and whispers, "You can do it. I am right here beside you." I feel safe and secure. I know everything will be all right because my mommy is with me.

My mom taught me that fear is a natural human emotion. Sometimes I am fearful if I feel unsafe or try something new. I fight fear with faith and believe I can do anything I put my mind to. That means getting the support of family and friends to help me when needed.

ROOM

When the weather starts to warm up in the spring, we plant flowers in the garden and rake the grass. I like to blow bubbles in the backyard with my mom. We plant roses and tulips that make our garden look beautiful. We decorate our garden with wind spinners, statues, and solar lights. We use wood chip mulch in the garden because it is an excellent source of nutrients for the soil.

In the summer, when it is really hot, we swim
in the backyard and eat ice cream sundaes. My
favourite ice cream is vanilla with chocolate syrup
and sprinkles on top. My mom loves Pralines and
Cream ice cream.

We also go hiking to exercise our bodies.
Hiking encourages me to test my limits and never
give up, no matter the challenges or struggles that
may arise. I am strong, brave and fieeeerce!

NEVER GIVE UP

In the fall, we collect leaves of all colors.
I like seeing shades of orange, yellow, red,
purple, and brown. The many colours remind
me of the rainbow.

We also go to the pumpkin patch and pick
the biggest pumpkin to make pumpkin pie. I really
like to eat the pumpkin seeds after my mom bakes
them and sprinkles salt on top.

We watch the snow fall from the sky in the winter. The snow on the tree branches, ground, and rooftop looks so beautiful. The snow looks like cotton balls gently placed on the ground.

I help my mom shovel the driveway, and we make a snowman and snow forts. We also drink hot chocolate in front of the fireplace.

Mommy and I do everything together, which brings me joy. I have my mommy, and my mommy has me. She is the best mommy. The best mommy that can ever be.

Everybody's family is special.
Some people live with their dad and mom,
or uncle, grandma, or grandpa. Some people
have stepmothers, stepfathers, or stepbrothers
or sisters. Love makes a family wonderful.

The End